100 Baby Days

One hundred **FUN** and **STIMULATING** activities for baby's first year

WRITTEN BY

Lisa Corti

Designed by Laura Walter

How to use this book

The activities in this book are set out in the order in which your baby is most likely to enjoy them, together with the most appropriate stage to try it — lying, sitting or crawling. Remember that every baby is unique and develops at their own pace, so don't worry if your little one isn't ready for a particular activity. Just move on to another and come back to it later.

GUIDE TO SENSORY CATEGORIES:

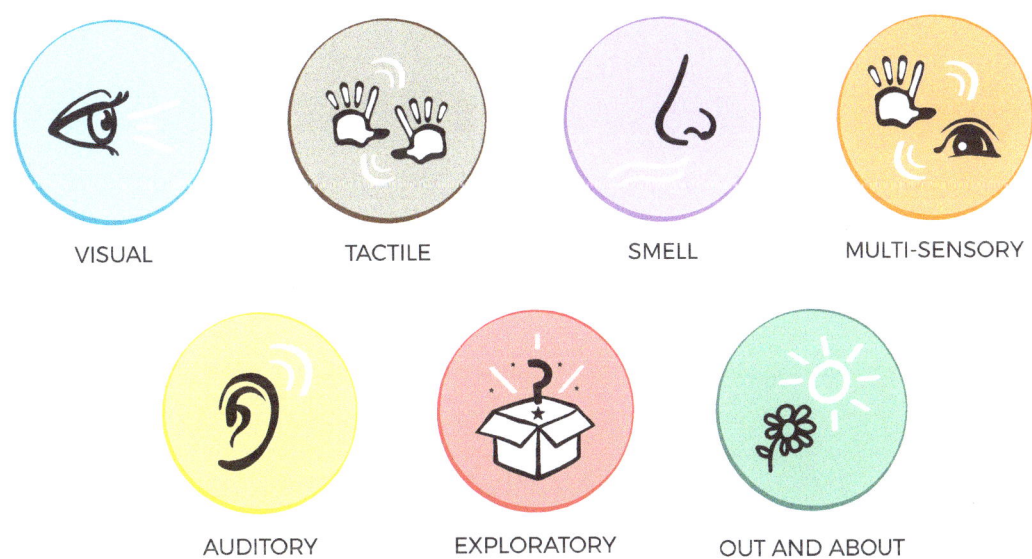

VISUAL

TACTILE

SMELL

MULTI-SENSORY

AUDITORY

EXPLORATORY

OUT AND ABOUT

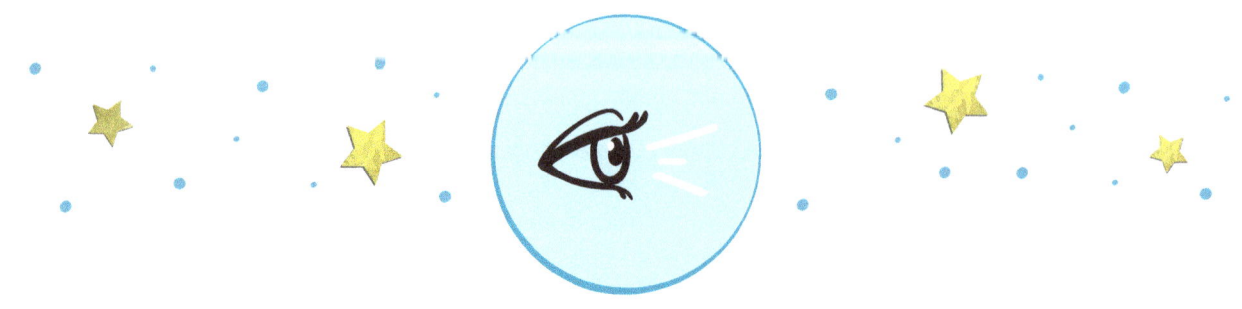

1. Bubbles!

Blow some bubbles.

2. Boogie time

Dance any baby blues away,
from disco to dervishes.

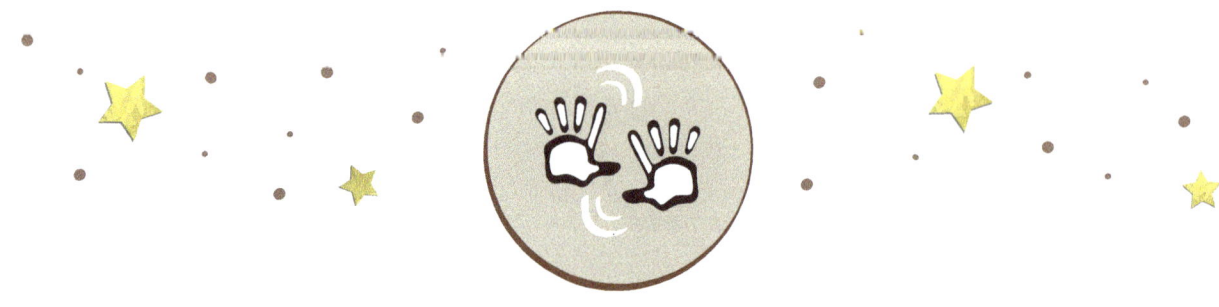

3. Relax

Try out simple
baby massage techniques.

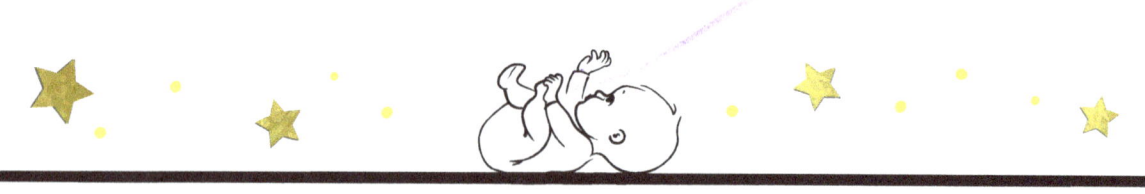

4. Tiny toes

Make hand and footprints
with baby-safe paint.

5. On the bus

Take a bus ride and watch
the world go by outside your window.

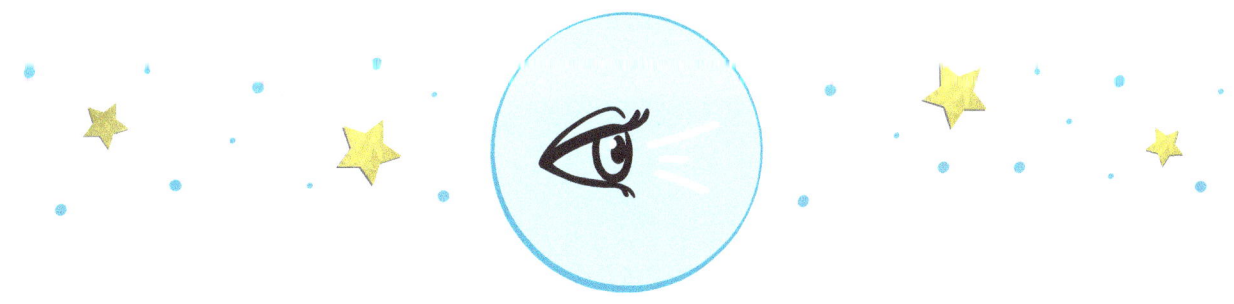

6. Peek-a-boo

Play peek-a-boo.

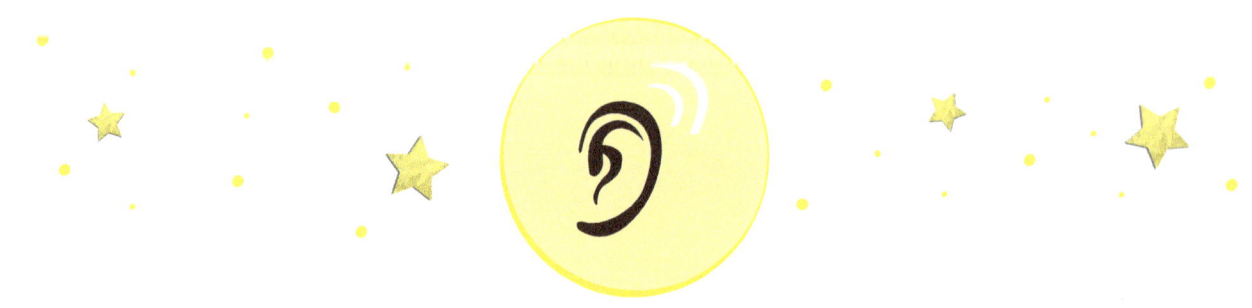

7. Karaoke

Sing, yodel, beat-box — anything goes!

8. Gentle nursery rhymes

Play Round and Round the Garden and This Little Piggy Went to Market.

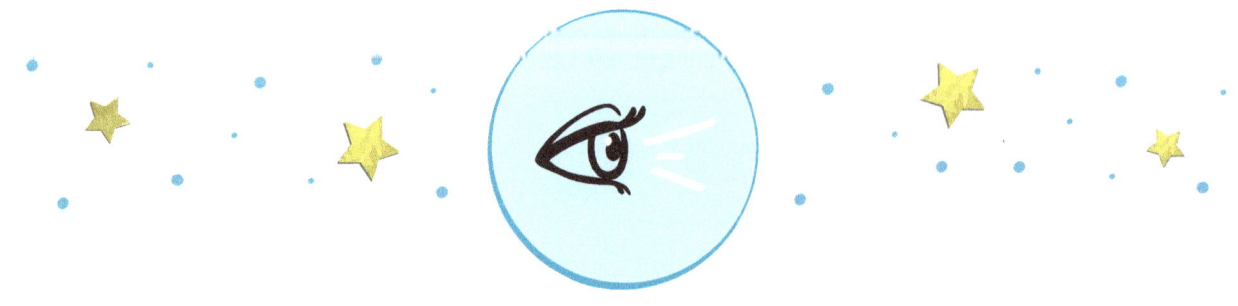

9. Picasso

Make a pattern book for baby
to look at, with bold, high-contrast
colours and shapes.

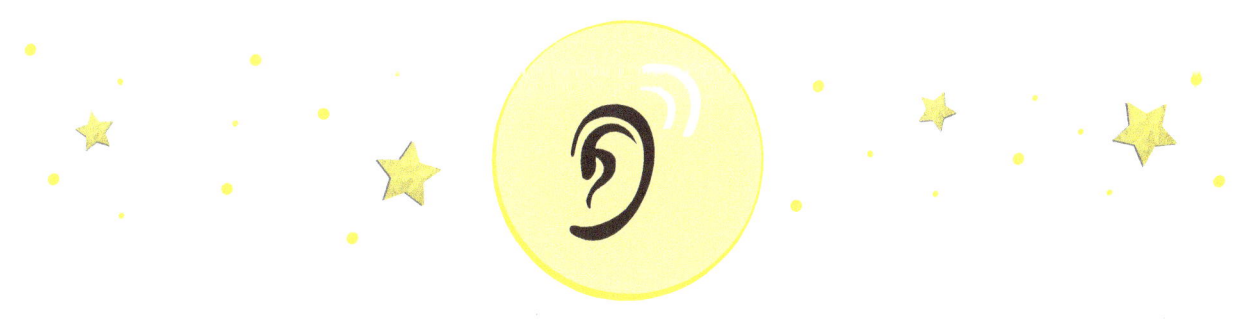

10. Indoor zoo

Do your best animal impressions
at full volume.

11. Giggle

Discover baby's tickliest spots.
Name each body part as you tickle.

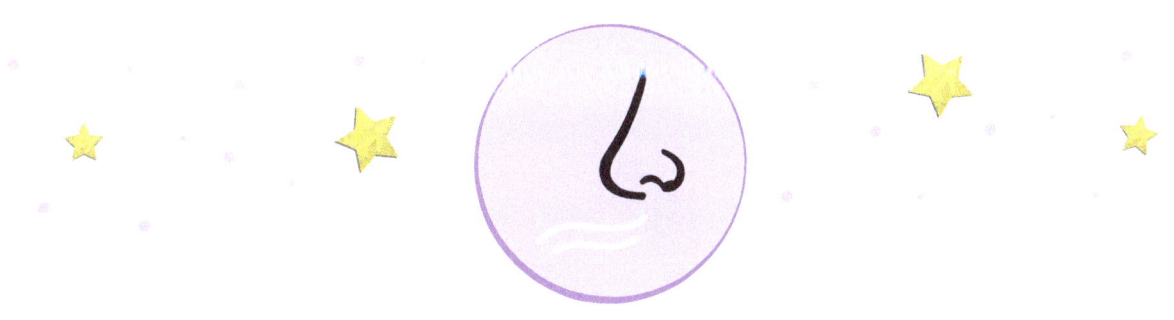

12. Smell the coffee!

Drizzle vanilla essence,
peppermint extract or coffee onto
an old handkerchief for baby to smell.

13. Fascinating fish

Visit an aquarium or aquatic shop.

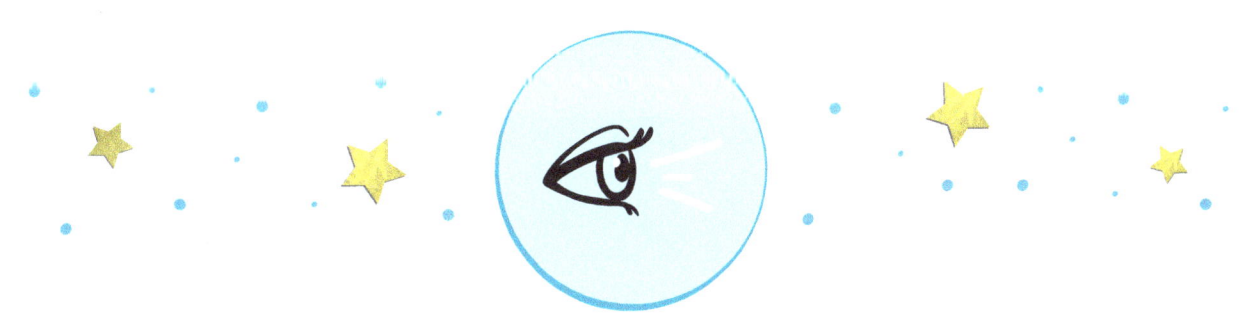

14. Plate faces

Draw silly faces on paper plates and place them on the wall by baby's changing mat.

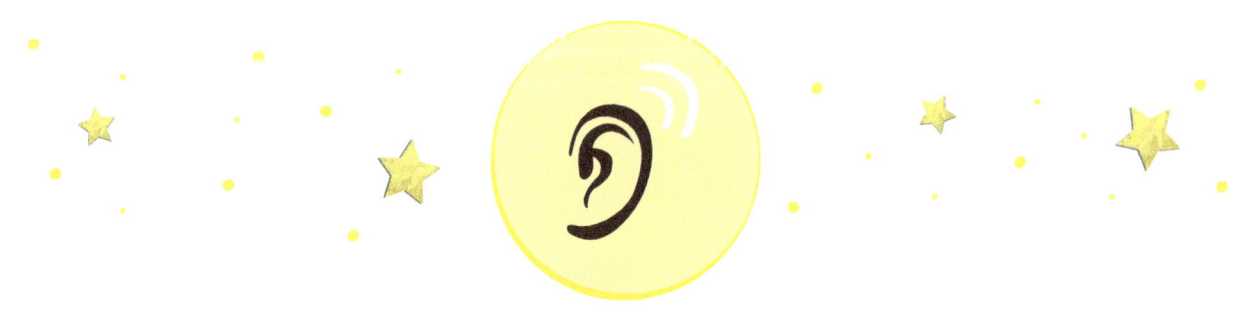

15. Spoon mobile

Hang teaspoons from a coat hanger to create a musical mobile.

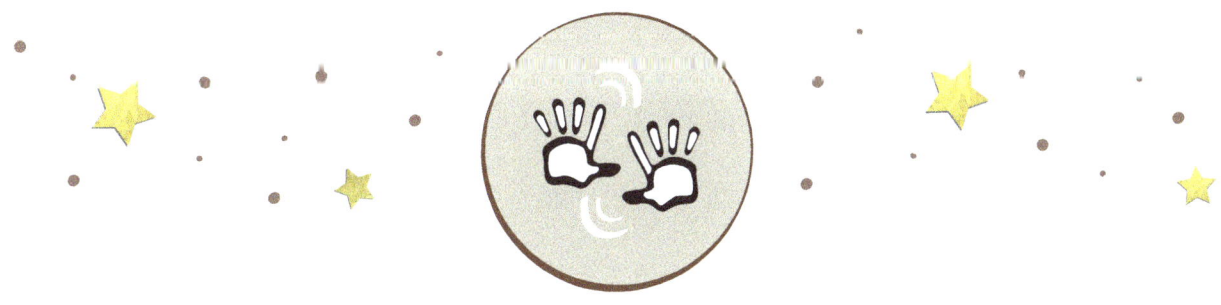

16. Sock monsters

Make a sock monster from an
old sock and make the creature
'nibble' baby's fingers and toes.

17. Son et Lumière

Turn off the lights, put on some music and dance a torch across the ceiling.

18. Old MacDonald

Visit a farm or zoo to see the animals,
or meet up with a friend who has
a mild-mannered pet.

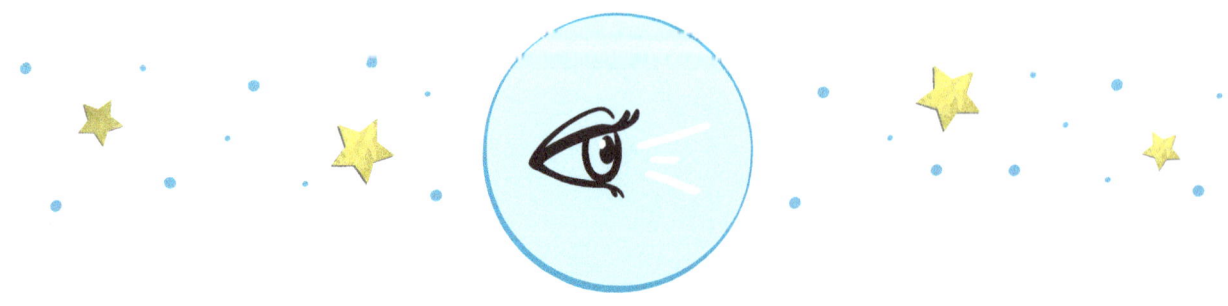

19. Disco baby

Hang a disco ball in front of a strong light source and set it spinning.

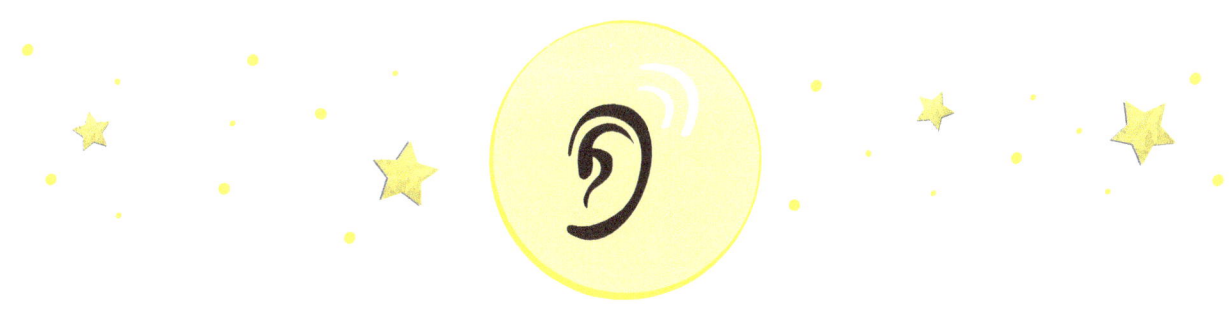

20. Shake, rattle and roll

Make a rattle using an empty
plastic bottle and dried pasta.
Seal tightly and check the seal often.

21. Spoon tails

Tie short pieces of string and ribbons
onto a wooden spoon handle.
Add knots or bows for extra interest.

22. At the beach

Blow up a beach inflatable and cover with blankets and toys.

23. Copy cat

Copy everything baby does,
from actions to sounds to
facial expressions.

24. Culture vulture

Take baby to a museum or art gallery with interactive exhibits and bright, bold displays.

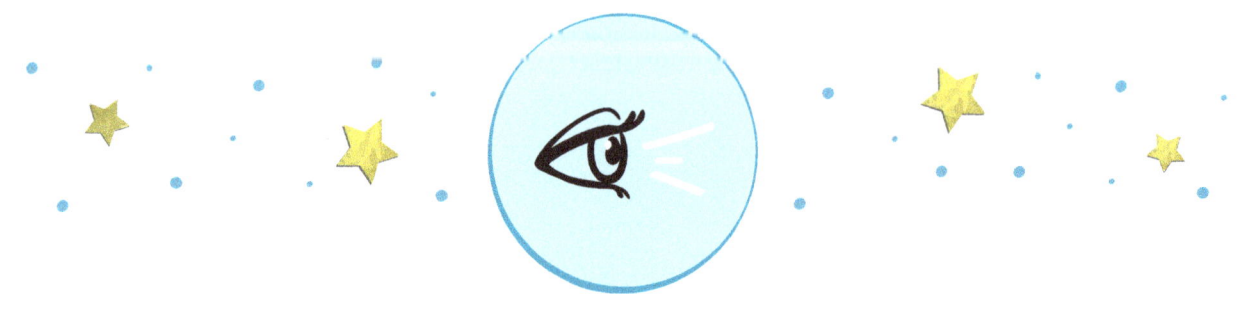

25. Punch and Judy

Put on a puppet show using
baby's favourite toys.

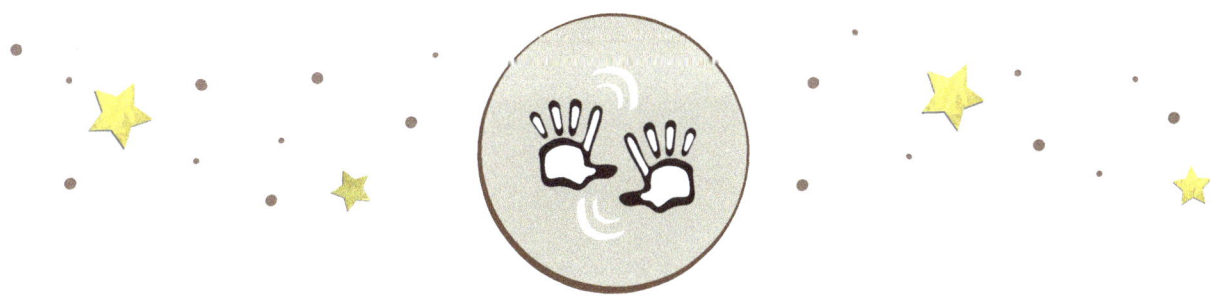

26. Scrap book

Make your own touchy-feely book with material scraps and craft supplies. Use non-toxic glue and stick down well.

27. Wibble wobble!

Holding firmly, sit baby on a
beach ball or yoga ball and roll them
gently from side to side.

28. Surprise!

Create a pop-up toy using a
wooden coffee stirrer or lollipop stick,
a yoghurt pot and baby's favourite toy.

29. Bon voyage

Watch trains or planes at
a station or airport.

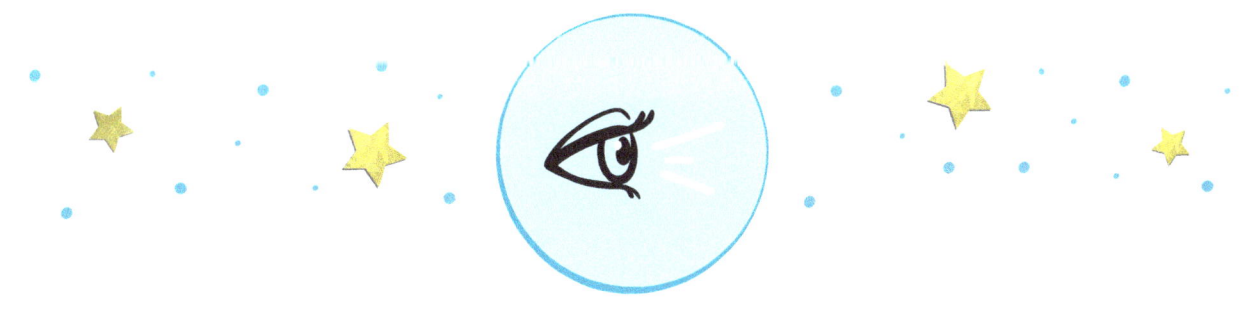

30. Balloon faces

Draw faces on balloons,
or create balloon octopuses with
ribbon tentacles to play with.

31. Action nursery rhymes

Sing action rhymes such as Humpty Dumpty, The Grand Old Duke of York, Horsey Horsey and Row, Row, Row your Boat.

32. A pinch of salt

Make soft, squidgy salt dough
to play with (1 cup flour, 1/2 cup salt,
1/2 cup water).

33. Movie star

Video baby playing and enjoying
activities throughout the day
and play it back to them.

34. Tower blocks

Build a tower out of plastic cups.
Count as you add each one to the top.

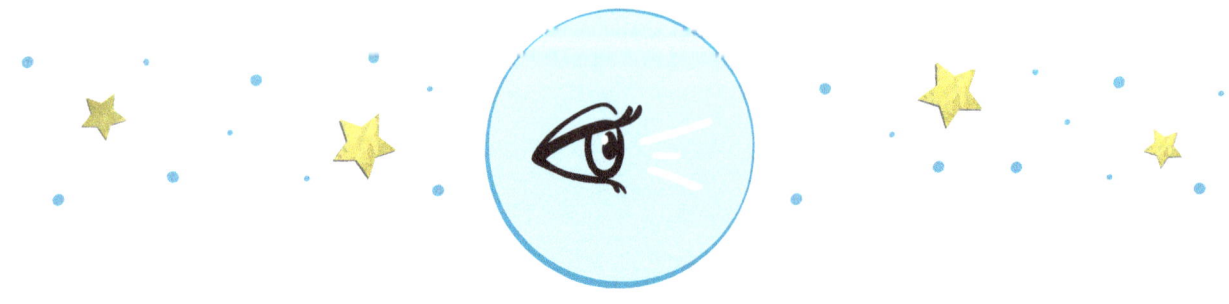

35. Mirror, mirror

Set up two baby-safe mirrors opposite each other for an infinity of reflections.

36. Crash, bang, wallop!

Make a drum kit out of saucepans and wooden spoons.

37. Wet, wet, wet

Lay out a towel and a shallow tray of water and make a splash!

38. Bopping balloons

Attach a balloon to baby's wrist using ribbon and an elastic hairband.

39. Big box, little box

Play with plastic containers
of different shapes and sizes.
Sort them, stack them, and see
which ones fit inside each other.

40. Off to market

Visit a fruit, veg or flower market.

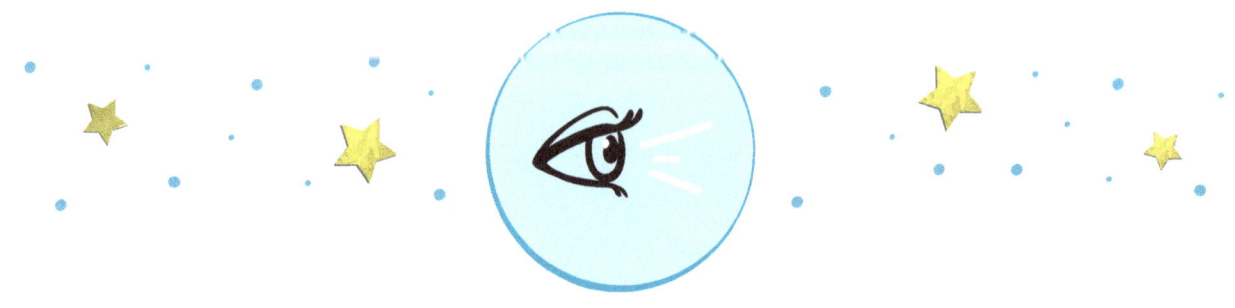

41. Paper helicopters

Download a template for paper helicopters from the internet and watch them spin.

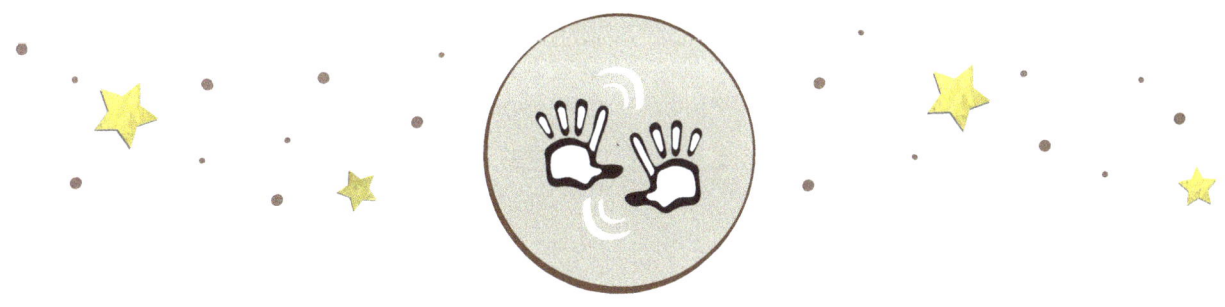

42. Achoo!

Fill a tissue box with socks and
let baby pull them out one by one.

43. Heaven scent

Visit a place with a distinctive smell, such as the seaside, lavender fields or a pine forest.

44. Box of tricks

Fill a box with unusual (but baby-safe) household items.

45. Rainy days

Pull on your wellies, grab an umbrella and go outside in the rain.

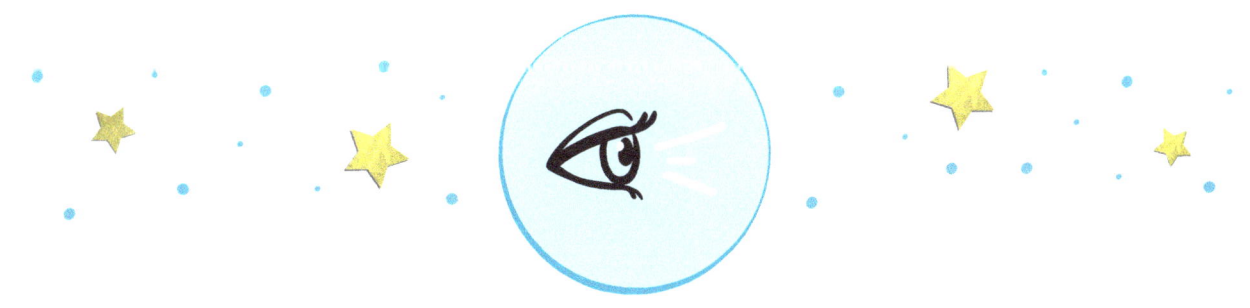

46. Shadow puppets

Make shadow puppets with
your hands and toys.

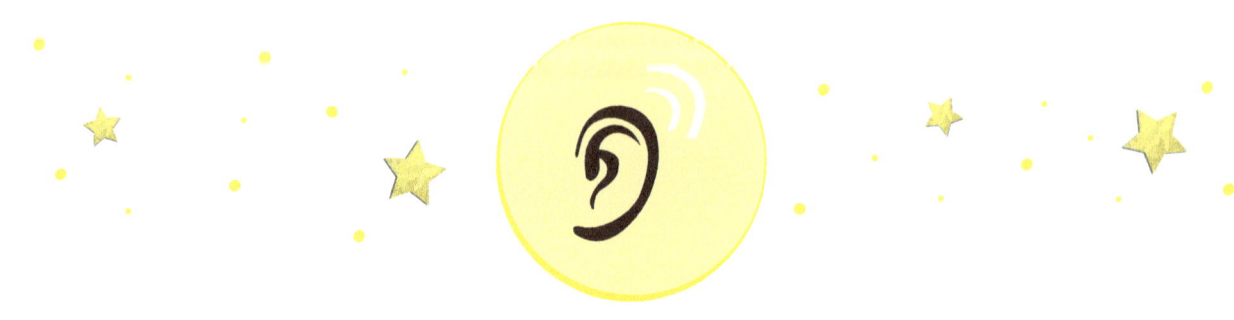

47. Oh là là!

Listen to foreign language songs
and nursery rhymes.

48. Spinning tops

Spin a biscuit-tin lid like a coin,
watching it rattle and roll to a stop.

49. Nose bags

Make fragrant beanbags by sewing
dried herbs or flowers into a sealed
pouch, or use fruity teabags as
a ready-made alternative!

50. Water baby

Find a swimming pool with a
fun toddler area, or set up a paddling
pool in the garden. Always supervise
baby near water.

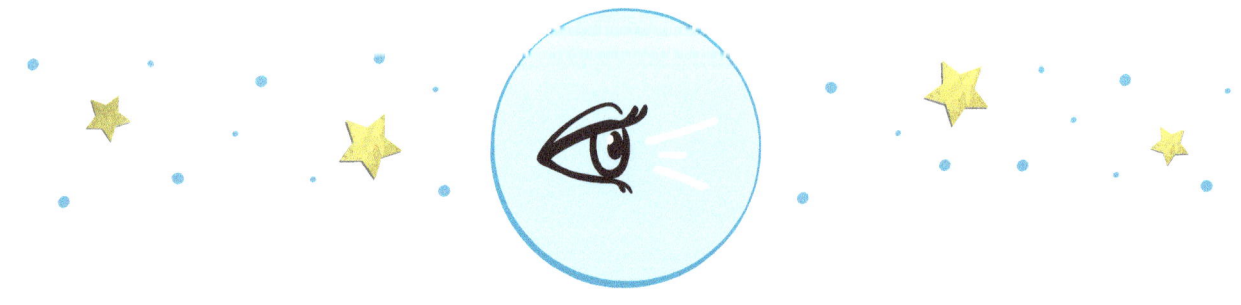

51. Twinkle, twinkle

Go out on a clear night and
show baby the moon and stars.

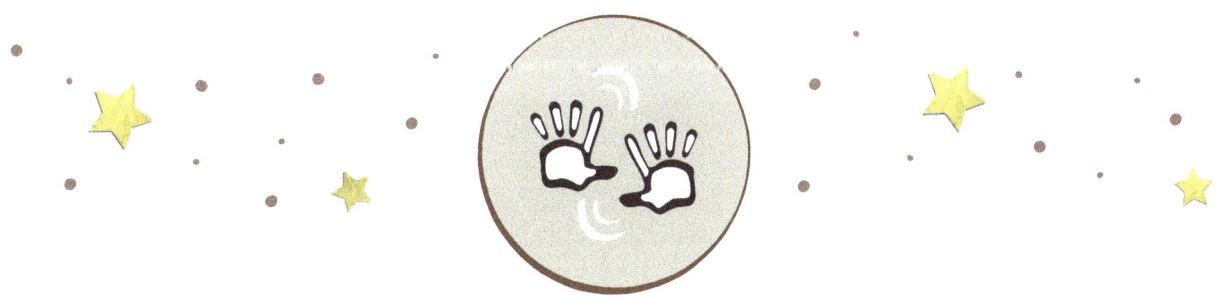

52. Spaghetti Western

Play with freshly cooked spaghetti.

53. Aeroplanes

Whoosh baby around the room, flying low over furniture and high above your head. Hold on tight!

54. Strike!

Play skittles using baby toys and a ball.

55. Park life

Watch ball games at a local park.

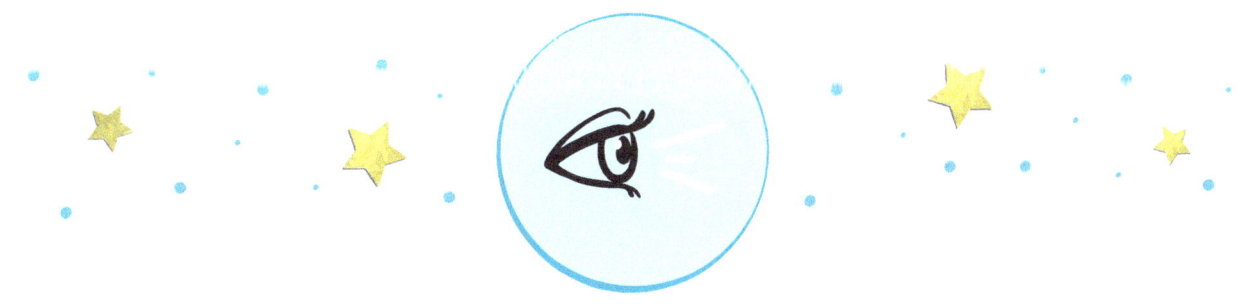

56. Wiggly worm

Cut a hole in a piece of card
and wiggle your finger through
it like a worm. Make it disappear,
then reappear.

57. Just for laughs

Watch YouTube clips of
other babies giggling.

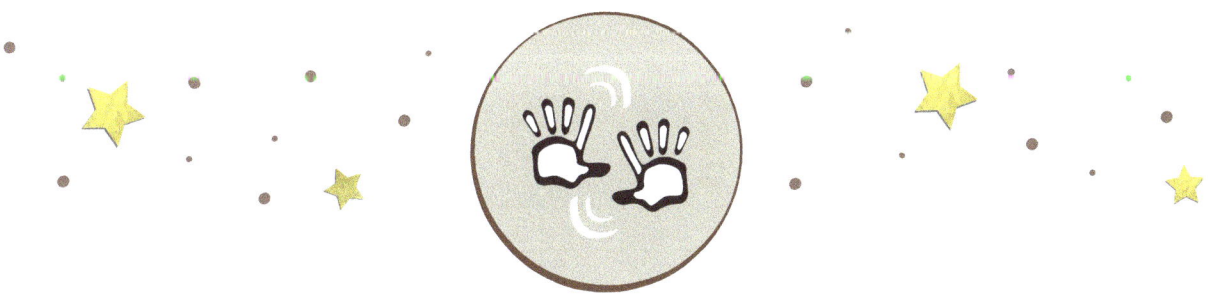

58. Straw man

Tie plastic drinking straws together
to create a 'straw man'.

59. Think inside the box

Sit baby in a large cardboard box.
Create 'letterboxes' to post
toys through.

60. Five little ducks

Feed the ducks at your local pond
or park, or hang a bird feeder
in the garden.

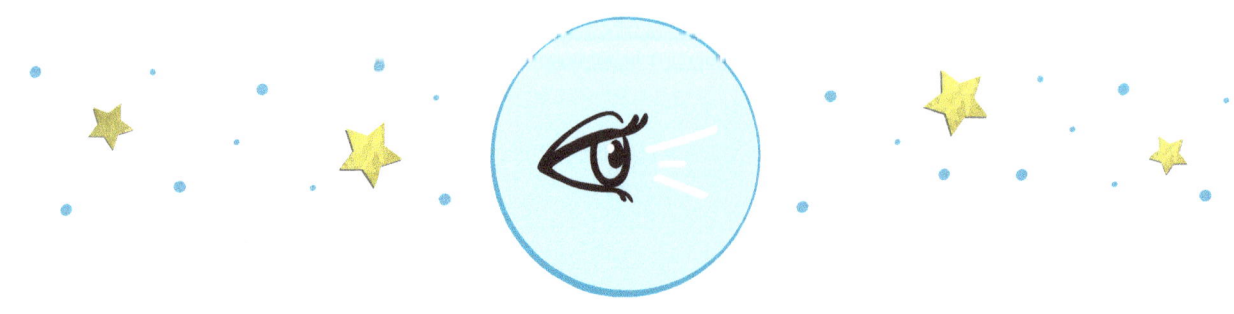

61. Dressing up box

Raid the wardrobe for silly hats, scarves and sunglasses. Dress up, and dress baby up. Pull silly faces and take fun selfies.

62. What's that noise?

Hide a squeaky toy under a cushion and ask baby to find it.

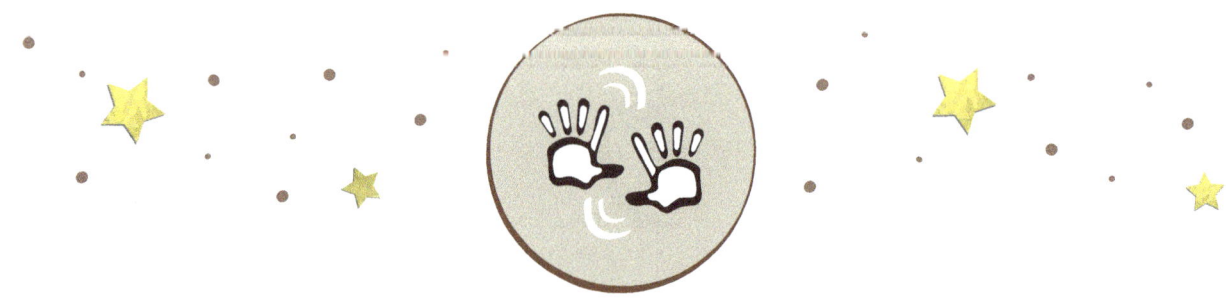

63. Paper chains

Make colourful paper chains
to play with.

64. Playtime

Use your arms as a swing, your legs as a slide and your knees as a bouncer to create an indoor playground.

65. Nature Walk

Take a walk through colourful, crunchy autumn leaves, or beautiful spring blossom.

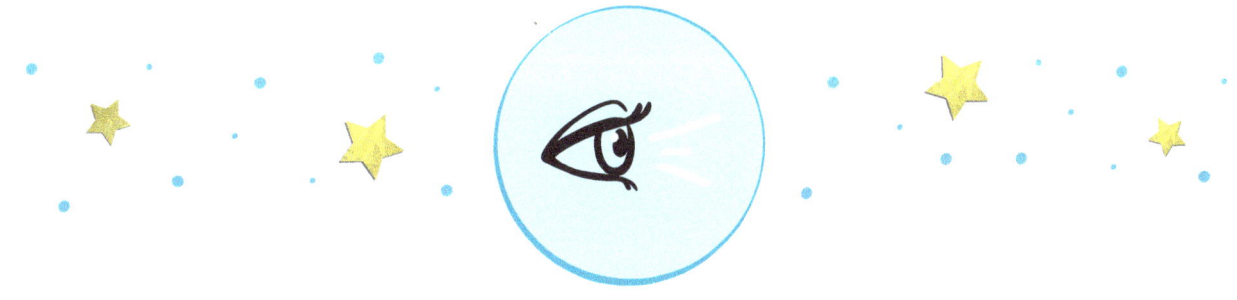

66. Incy wincy

Make a 'spider' out of string or wool.
Make it scuttle across the floor or
disappear up a kitchen roll 'drainpipe'.

67. Pat-a-cake

Play clapping games
such as pat-a-cake.

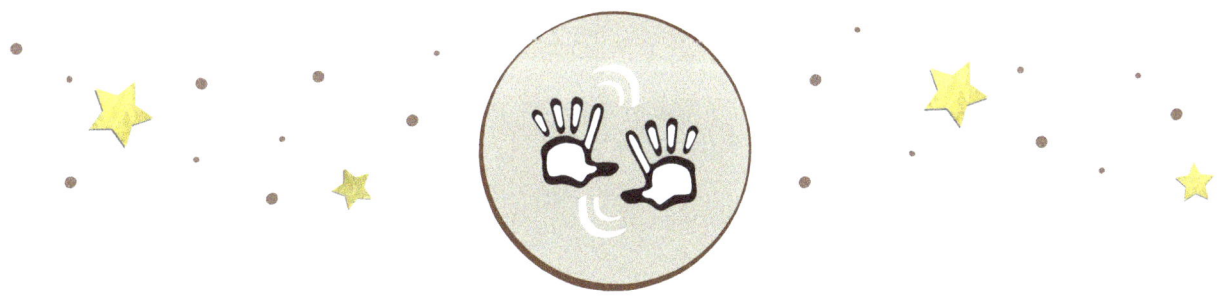

68. At the greengrocers

Play with a potato (yes, really!)
and other baby-safe fruit and veg.

69. Bags of fun

Make a squishy, sparkly sensory bag by putting glitter, washing up liquid and water into a zip-top sandwich bag. Seal well with packaging tape.

70. Bookworm

Visit the children's section of
your local library.

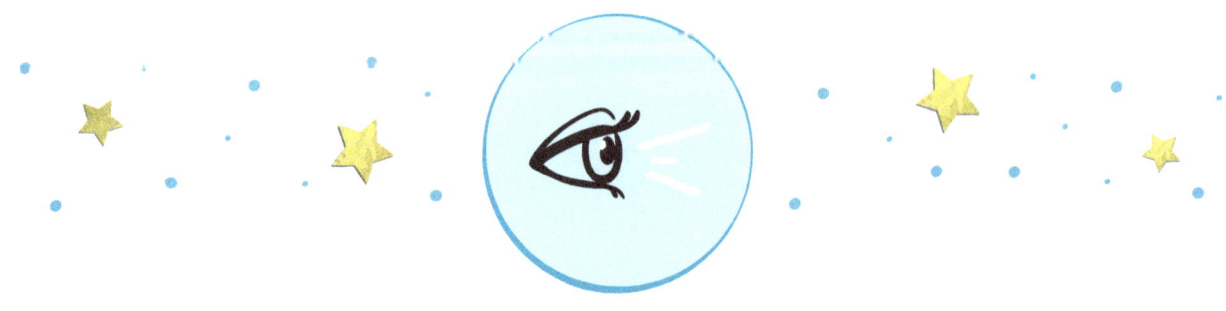

71. My family and friends

Print out and laminate photos
of baby's friends and relatives, or make
a photobook. Name each person
as you show them to baby.

72. Read all about it

Rip, tear and scrunch an
old newspaper.

73. All washed up

Scoop foamy washing-up
liquid bubbles onto a paper plate
and let baby play.

74. Washing day

Sit baby in front of a spinning washing machine, let them sort the sock pile, or tie toys to the laundry basket.

75. A present for me?

Wrap baby's toys in old paper
and help 'unwrap' them.

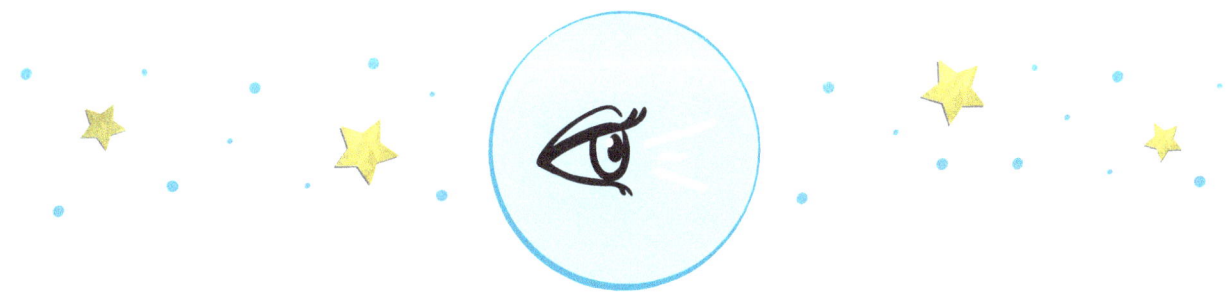

76. Smile!

Set up a seasonal photo shoot.
Use a white sheet as a backdrop and
extra lighting for a professional look.

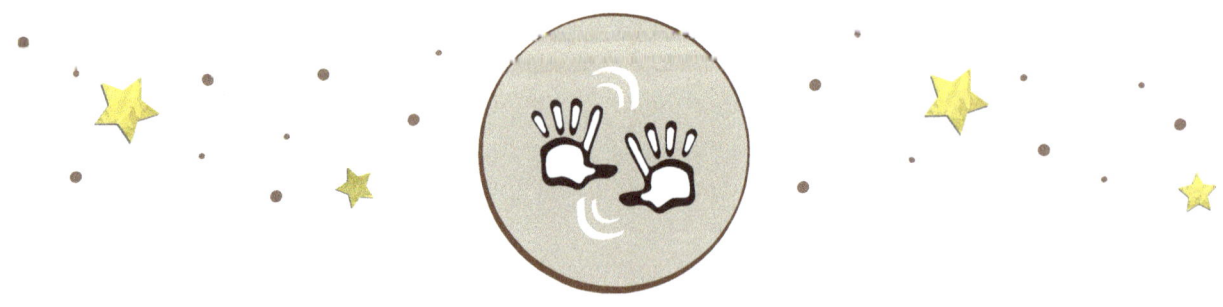

77. Spider's web

Thread plastic bottle tops on string and criss-cross between chair legs to make a spider's web. Tie firmly and dismantle when done.

78. Whizz kid

Download a baby-game app on
your smartphone or tablet.

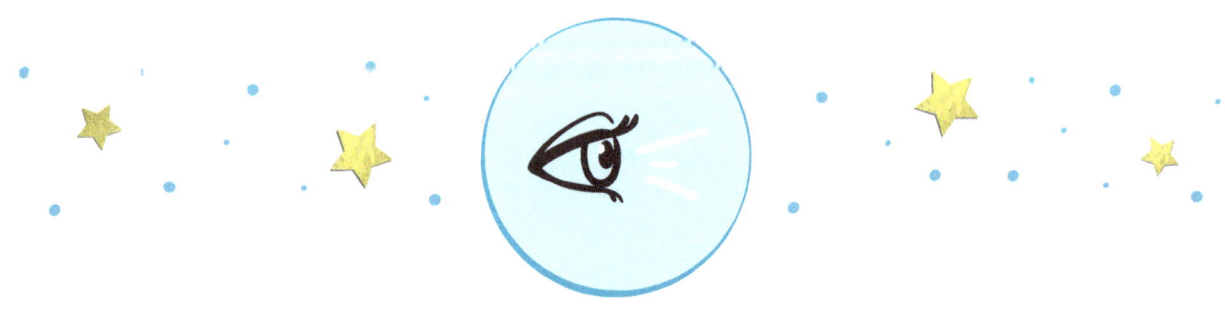

79. Magician's cups

Hide a small toy under one of three cups. Move them around and play 'Where's the toy?'.

80. Rhythm and blues

Beat out different rhythms — fast and slow, long and short, loud and soft.

81. Boïng!

Tie a soft toy to a table leg
with a short piece of elastic.

82. Baa Baa (pink) sheep

Let baby play with a ball
of brightly-coloured wool.
Watch closely to make sure
baby doesn't get tangled up.

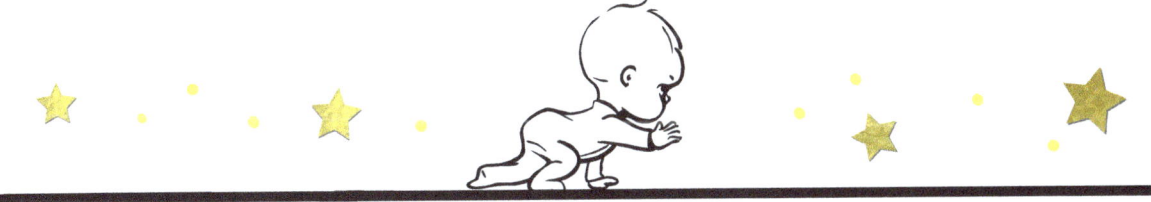

83. Shh, it's a secret!

Create a secret den under
a table using sheets and blankets.

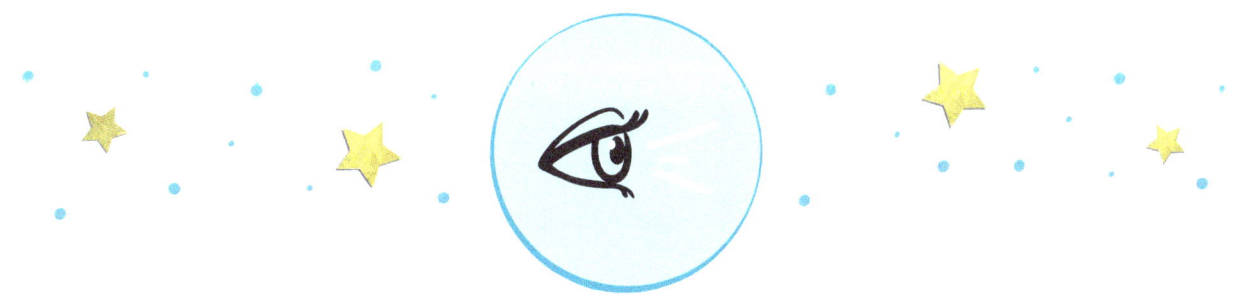

84. What's in my pocket?

Hide toys in different pockets
and help baby find them all.

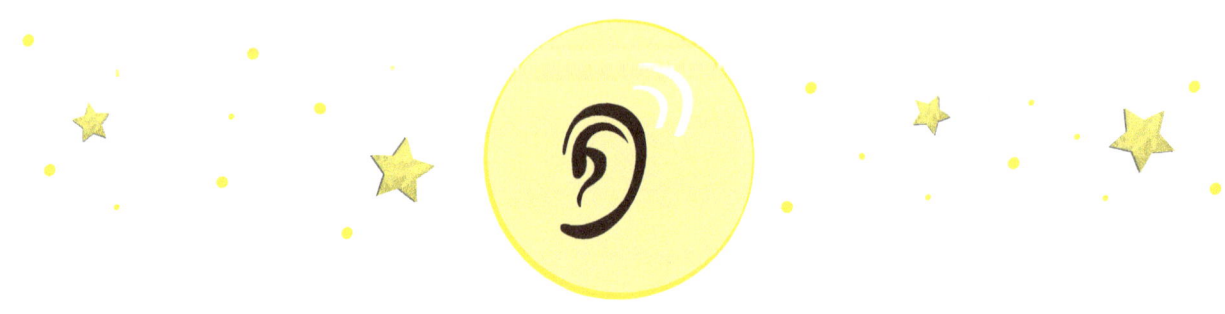

85. Spoken word

Say tongue twisters, recite rhymes or make up exciting stories involving family and friends.

86. Slime!

Create a gloopy, gooey slime using one-part water to two-parts cornflour.

87. Trapped!

Tuck a favourite toy inside a kitchen whisk for baby to puzzle out.

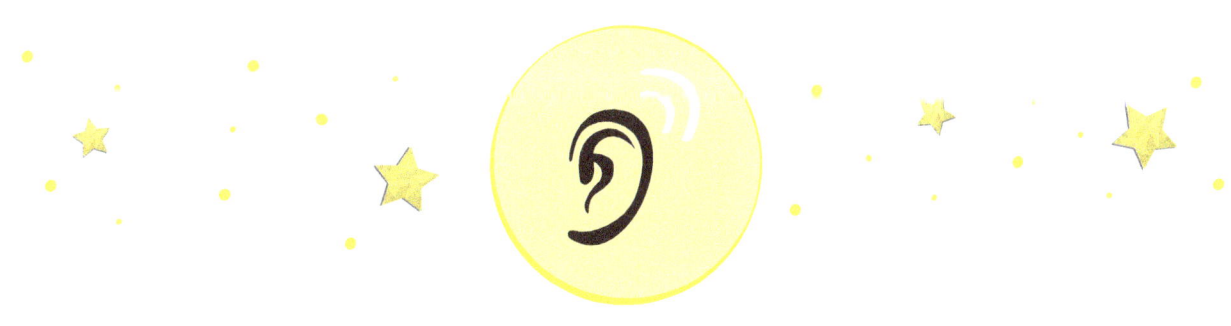

88. Talk, talk

Make a telephone with two yoghurt
pots and a length of string.
Talk in silly voices.

89. Patchwork carpet

Spread different textures
such as silk scarves, fluffy rugs
and rubber mats on the floor
for baby to crawl over.

90. Spice it up

Add mild spices to meals.
Before serving, mix a pinch with
water and rub onto a tissue
for baby to smell.

91. Assault course

Create ramps, tunnels and obstacles using seat cushions, pillows and boxes.

92. Teddy bears' picnic

Take lunch or dinner outside and have a picnic with baby's favourite cuddly toys.

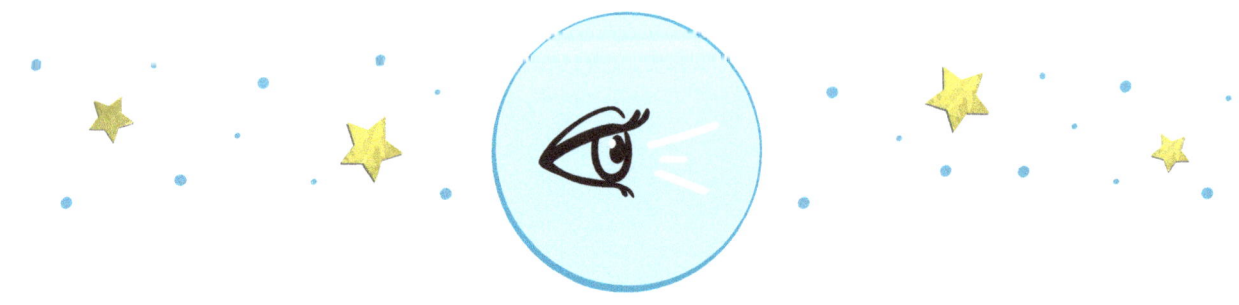

93. Curtain call

Hide behind a curtain or chair and call for baby to find you.

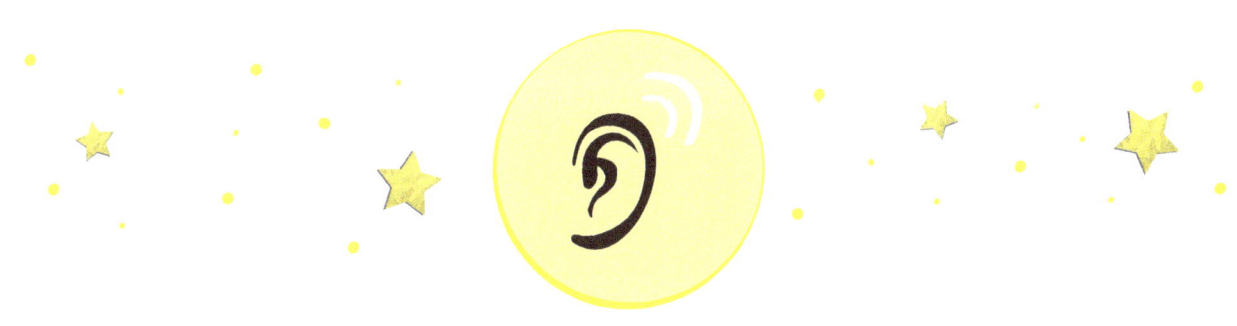

94. Twang!

Stretch rubber bands across a plastic container for a homemade guitar.

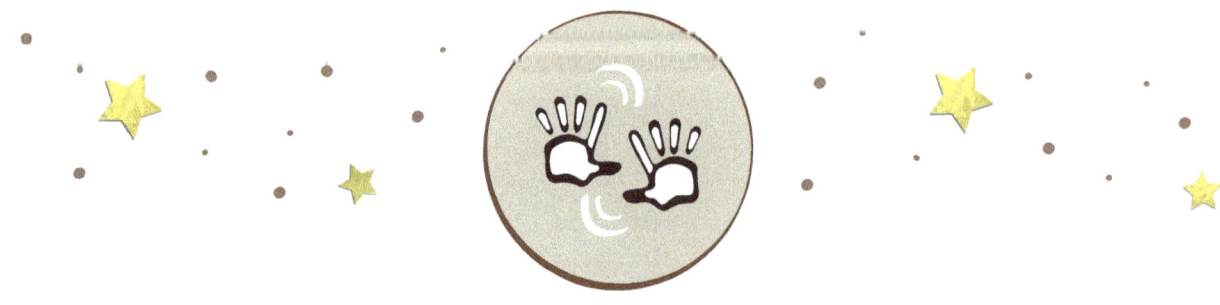

95. Opposites attract

Play with contrasting textures —
warm and cold, wet and dry,
rough and smooth.

96. Mind the gap

Make a tunnel with your legs and encourage baby to crawl through it. Make the gap smaller so they have to squeeze through.

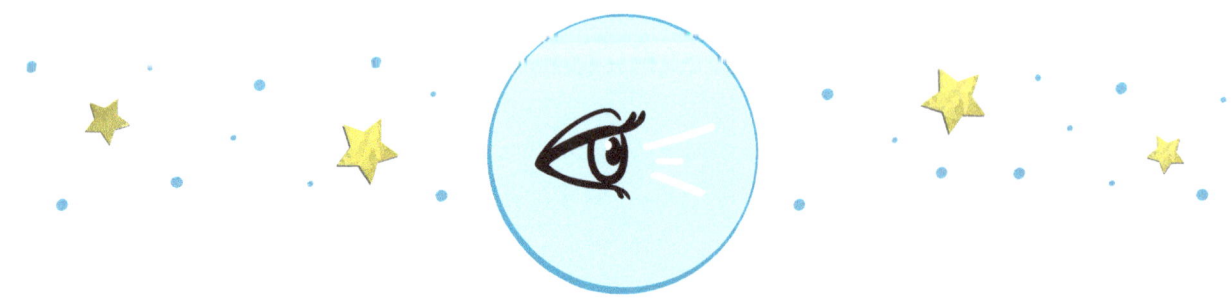

97. Water art

Use water and a sponge or chunky paintbrush to make patterns on a stone path outside.

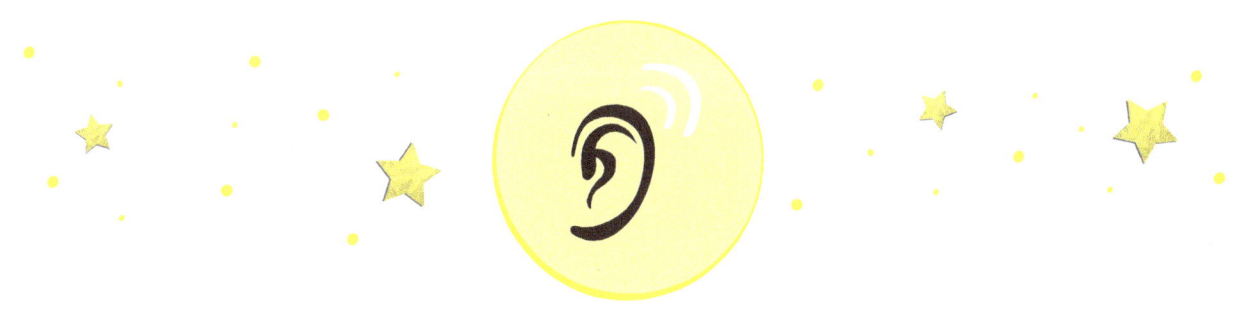

98. Clickety-clack

Thread milk bottle tops and yoghurt
pots onto a piece of string for
a clattering pull-along toy.

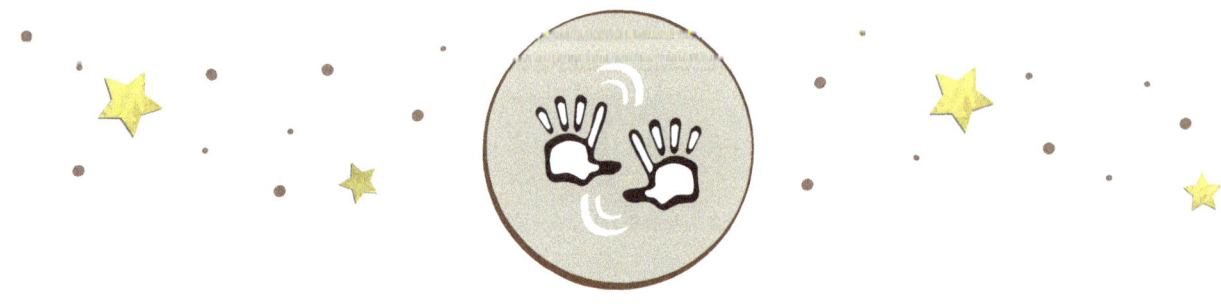

99. Tickle chase

Chase baby on hands and knees.
Tickle them whenever
you catch them.

100. Just cruisin'

Set chairs, side tables or boxes a small distance apart. Encourage baby to cruise between them.

We'd love to hear about the *fun* you've had with *your little one*, sharing the activities in this book.

Upload your photos and share your baby days at <u>facebook.com/100babydays</u> or follow us on:

#100BabyDays